LET'S HAVE A BITE!

A Banquet of Beastly Rhymes

By Robert L. Forbes

Drawings by Ronald Searle

Overlook Duckworth
New York · London

First published in the United States in 2010 by
Overlook Duckworth, Peter Mayer Publishers, Inc.
New York and London

NEW YORK:
141 Wooster Street
New York, NY 10012
www.overlookpress.com

LONDON:
Duckworth & Co. Ltd.
Greenhill House
90-93 Cowcross Street
London EC1M 6BF
www.ducknet.co.uk

Text has been set in ITC Berekley Old Style

Cataloging-in-Publication Data is available from the Library of Congress.

Book design and type formatting by Bernard Schleifer
Manufactured in China
1 3 5 7 9 8 6 4 2
ISBN 978-1-59020-409-2 (US)
ISBN 978-0-71563-984-9 (UK)

For Miguel, Forever
The Best Son Ever

CONTENTS

The Chocolate Bunny 7

Naughty Lion Cubs 8

Hugh the Emu 10

Fiji Monkey Business 13

The Zoo VIP (Very Idle Panda) 14

Natty Nat 16

The Story of Rory 19

Flick the Fly 21

Clair the All-Seeing Seal 22

Buffalo Biff 24

Ooh, Lala! 27

Rubber Ducky 28

The Turtle Dash 30

Theodore's Great Pitch 32

A Wheeler-Dealer 34

Daniel Spaniel 37

A Crocodile's Wiles 39

Shauna   40

Baker Betty   43

A Busy Day for Goslings   45

Tardy Tammy   50

A Vole Hole   53

The Rhino's Wine   54

Biggie Dog and Little Pup   58

The Houseguest   61

Bad Andy Bear   63

Doozer of the Deep   66

Bug Thugs   69

Mean Cuisine   70

Il Gatto   73

The Inchworm Sprint   74

The Tickling Dingo   76

Funny Bunny   78

THE CHOCOLATE BUNNY

The Chocolate Bunny ate a lemon drop
Thinking it would help his hop.
It gave him bounce but his next litter
Of chocolate bunnies tasted bitter.
He left Ye Olde Candy Shoppe
Convinced the drops made him a flop.

A bitter bunny then was bought
By a customer who thought
This is quite a tangy treat!
Dark and edgy, not too sweet!

Business at the Candy Shoppe
Started then to boom non-stop.
Sweet is neat, but bitter's neater
For the savvy chocolate eater.
Our bunny then bounced back to work
With a new digestive quirk:
He and his milk chocolate Missus
Now only smooch with lemondrop kisses!

NAUGHTY LION CUBS

Otto and Lark are naughty!
When one is caught he
Blames the other,
"Mom, it's my brother!
Can't you see?
It wasn't me!"
Oh, Lark and Otto!
Moms always know
Who did what
And who did not.
Because one got caught
The other ought
Not then to say
"I got away!"

Otto and Lark
Have to face Dad
Who gets roaring mad
Because they were bad,
And what is worst,
Get no dessert!

Can they be good
As they should?
No way! Next day,
Onward they go—
Lark and Otto
Twins in trouble—
"Off to your room!
On the double!"

HUGH THE EMU

What do you do with a blue emu named Hugh?
You say, "Hey, Hugh—come out to play!"
He can chase you, race you
And outpace you.
Hugh is fast—a real blast!
He's behind you, then he's past you!

On rainy days, inside,
Hugh gives you a ride.
You can explore
Behind every door,
Search for more
Adventure when you enter
Each room and zoom
Around
The world you've found.

Even blue emus
Need to snooze,
So off he goes,
And, who knows?
Hugh may be back
With a coat of black.

What hue might he borrow
When Hugh comes tomorrow?
What if he had a golden tail,
Pale like ginger ale?
Is he a different fellow
If his feathers are yellow?
Do you think
He'll be brown or pink?
Or, what a sight
If he's purple and white!
Or yipes!
He could be in stripes!
Or maybe he'll come back to you
An emu of a dark deep blue.

You two
Can decide what next to do.
And I'm so happy for you and Hugh,
Your emu of blue.
But can I play, too?

FIJI MONKEY BUSINESS

A monkey in Fiji named Gigi
Sits up high up in her palm tree
Where from the top she calmly lets drop
Cocoanuts on the golfers below.

She gleefully ruins the play
Of dogs on their holiday.
The nuts make the mutts miss all their putts—
What a doggone funny show!

THE ZOO VIP
(VERY IDLE PANDA)

The Giant Panda at the zoo
Just sits and chomps
On fresh bamboo,
His belly like a cooking pot,
Which happens when you eat a lot.
He's content to do not much but chew.
Which is all he seems to do
(That and poo!).

A celebrity ball
Of white and black—
Once you've seen him,
Why ever go back?

NATTY NAT

I know a narwhal named Nat
Who wears a thick woolen hat
In winter's ice and storm
To keep his cue-ball head warm.

When the spring sun brings the thaw
He sports a hat of straw,
A rakish panama
That drives the girls gaga.

(In the summer he needs no topper—
His groovy shades are a real show-stopper.)

For fall, it's old-style tweedy—
Nat's scarf a little seedy,
Tied on his tusk like a country gent,
With a splash of musky scent.

Those jaunty get-ups that I'd call artful
Make our Nat the Best-Dressed Narwhal.

THE STORY OF RORY

Rory the rattler,
My slithery friend,
You fill most people with fear.
They don't consider
That to mother
Even you were dear.

She taught you the ropes
Of desert life,
And how to spring into battle:
First tense your coil,
Next, bare your fangs
Then wildly wiggle your rattle.

The Rory I love
Would only strike
When cornered or surprised
But he lies in the sun
Like a loaded six-gun—
That's why he's so despised.

Just let Rory know you're coming
By humming a catchy old song.
He'll pick up the tune and happily croon—
His tail keeping time right along.

FLICK THE FLY

Flick the fly
Is no nice guy,
A huge but tiny pest.
He'll buzz my head
Until he's fed—
Never giving me a rest.

Flick swims a loop
In my beet soup
Or dances on a leaf of lettuce,
And then he'll say
In his cocky way,
"No swatting—where does that get us?"

I try to smack him,
Strive to whack him—
But, worn out, surrender—
Knowing that he
Got the best of me,
A defeated dinner defender.

When sated, he'll say—
"I'm on my way,
And tomorrow, let's have some beef."
My goodness, what gall,
In one so small,
An appallingly impudent thief.

The very next day,
I'll be chopping away
Preparing a memorable feast
Knowing full well,
At the dinner bell
I'll be sharing it with that beast.

CLAIR THE ALL-SEEING SEAL

Clair gazed into her crystal ball
Proclaiming she could see it all,
Not just what, but also when
And she was right (now and again.)

She'd predict when schools of fishes
Swimming thick, cold, delicious—
Would be headed for the seals
Who snapped them up with grunts and squeals.

Clair could say on which dark nights
The sky would blaze with northern lights
And sadly she could always tell
Which pal a killer whale would fell.

Carved from ice, her crystal ball
Worked through winter, spring, and fall.
But in the summer, what a muddle—
It would melt into a puddle.

To help All-Seeing Clair to bridge
The warmer months she bought a fridge
To keep her ice-ball cold and clear
And her visions sharp all year.

So, hungry seals, recall next time
You find yourselves in a polar clime
And want to know just when and where
To catch a meal—go see our Clair.

BUFFALO BIFF

A buffalo I know named Biff—
A devilish Yellowstone dandy—
Will snort and stalk away if
You don't have your camera handy.

His great grandfather, Bull Hickle
Had such a striking presence
They engraved him on the nickel—
An American legend for five cents.

Young Biff carries on the tradition:
By giving each carload The Pose,
For which you don't need his permission—
He's a ham from head to toes.

But ornery Biff isn't a pet,
So take your pix, stay in the car,
And show your respect
For a genuine Wild West star.

OOH, LALA!

My friend Lala,
A cuddly-snuggly koala,
Lives at the zoo.
Kids think she is cute
But it's not true!
Lala is a nasty brute.

When she spies her keeper she spits,
And throws tantrums and fits
If her dinner is not what she wants,
Or the weather's too stormy for jaunts.

Lala is not a nice girl at all!
Why ever, then, would I call
Her a friend—this bratty fuzz-ball
Of the zoo?
Well, kids, I'm a bad koala, too!

RUBBER DUCKY

My rubber ducky
Bathes with me
And boy does my ducky
Ever see
How bad I can be
So I took out
His squawky squeakee –
Now he
Can't squeal on me.

THE TURTLE DASH

In the town of Fair-Dinkum-on-Ash
They hold an annual bash
Where the prize is a neat pile of cash
For winning the hundred yard dash.

With many a cut and a gash
Their shells tumble up in a hash
While they run as though stung by a lash,
And the racers end up in a mash
From trying maneuvers too rash!

The turtles compete for a sash
So you bet the behavior is brash!
And this year the winner was Crash
Who rounded the course in a flash!

The teeth of the turtles did gnash
As Crash gave a shove and a slash
That set off the final grand smash
And let him go home with the stash,
Leaving others to clean up the trash.

His boast to the crowd made a splash:
"Next year all you dashers I'll thrash!"

THEODORE'S GREAT PITCH

Theodore the lemur
Goes door to door
Selling boar bristle brushes.
He can sell—just as well—
Brooms of husks and rushes.

A tidy guy, he looks shy,
But before you've realized
His eyes, that voice,
Leave you no choice—
You've been hypnotized.

So take care, please beware
Of a lemur at your door,
Or you'll consume
A brush or a broom—
Bewitched by Theodore.

A WHEELER-DEALER

My friend Iggy,
A little guinea piggy,
Eats nuts and fruit.

With happy squeaks
He fills his cheeks—
It looks so cute!

But that's enough!
Now off your duff!
Climb onto your wheel!

Round you go,
You ball of dough—
To earn your next meal.

DANIEL SPANIEL

I know a spaniel whose name is Daniel.
He came to say, "Come out and play—
Let's have a run and get some sun!"
My mom said, "Go – I know you know
You won't go far, my superstar."
"I'll be alright and stay in sight,"
I said to mom to make her calm
And not to worry so I could hurry
After Dan. Off he ran
Around the tree and back to me.
"Catch me, catch me, if you can," said speedy Dan.

He's fast as you please so I catch a breeze.
Together we fly like birds in the sky
Or fall to the ground and tumble around.
After we've played we rest in the shade
And tell tall stories of spaniel glories.

Then time for a snack, we both head back.
Mom welcomes us home. "How far did you roam
On your travels today, and what did you play?"
My mother will say.
She laughs at our tales of swallows and snails
And secret places and who won our races.

My victory lap must end in a nap,
But I say to Dan, "Come back if you can
That's when we'll run again!"

A CROCODILE'S WILES

When a crocodile smiles or a crocodile cries
You have to wonder what crock of old lies
He's hatching between his crocodile ears
And the eyes that are flowing with crocodile tears.

Who knows what's brewing inside of his head?
(Or is it his appetite that's smiling instead?)
Don't wait to find out, for he'll take it amiss
If you try to refuse his crocodile kiss.

SHAUNA

A chicken-stewing cat named Shauna
Slipped on her sweat in the sauna.
She moaned on the floor,
"I must reach the door,
Or I'll be a fricasseed goner!"

BAKER BETTY

Betty Baboon is a baker
Who makes piles of cookies and pies.
When she put lots of stuff in
Her ten-berry muffin,
She won the Gold Homemaking Prize.

A BUSY DAY FOR GOSLINGS

Lined up one after the other,
They waddle quickly after mother.
Pip, Pop, Peep and Squeak,
Now follow Momma to the creek,
First time seeing water,
Son, son, son, daughter.

"It's time for you to learn to swim—
Watch your Daddy, eyes on him.
Stay in line, keep it neat,
Paddle with your webby feet.
Follow me, around we go,
Paddle hard, paddle slow.
Then back to shore, out you hop,
Peep and Squeak and Pip and Pop.

"Time for lunch—
Some grain to munch.
In the shade, we'll have a rest.
No swimming now, your mom knows best.
Later in the summer day
To the creek we'll make our way
To have another cooling dip—
Pop and Peep and Squeak and Pip."

Yellow, fluffy, float along
With a little goosie song
"Sun is warm and gives us light
To swim and feed before the night
When we rest and have our sleep,"
Sing Squeak and Pop and Pip and Peep.
Momma says, "For now, enough,
My darling little balls of fluff!
Out you get! Shake off the water,
Son, son, son, and daughter.

A little supper, then to bed,
Each fuzzy yellow sleepy head,
Snuggled in the warm goose nest.
Mom and Daddy also rest.
"Good night, goslings, one by one.
Daughter, son and son and son."

TARDY TAMMY

Tammy Tiger, always late,
Lost a load of time
But always said when she grew up,
The clock she'd learn to mind.

Papa Tiger gave her a watch
To wear on a dainty paw,
"Now Tammy," he said,
"It glows in the dark—
The hour you can't ignore."

But Tammy forgot,
Paying no heed,
And let the watch unwind.
It got too late
For a hunting date,
No fresh prey could she find.

By hunger sapped, Tammy was trapped
And shipped off to the zoo
Where every day, at ten past one,
They served her all she could chew.

No more missed dates for this big cat,
No more skipping a meal,
And no more freedom, but she doesn't care—
How would you like that deal?

A VOLE HOLE

Moe Vole
Dug a hole
And said,
"Time for bed."
His dream?
Ice cream.
Next day
He'll play
With frisky voles
From other holes.
After rest
Comes the best—
Every vole
Gets a bowl.
Bug blood ice cream:
Moe's dream!
His came true—
Some bug blood ice cream
For you?

THE RHINO'S WINE

Amos the rhinoceros
Makes wine
Tenderly tending
Each vine.
He makes red, white, and rosé.

His harvest can be great, bad, or ok;
The juicy weight the grapes will gain
Depends on the sun and rain.
In spring, there's cutting and pruning.
Bad bugs do a good job of ruining
The leaves, vines, and ripe fruit
So he sprays to give them the boot.

Summer is the growing phase
As the grapes sunward gaze.
Too much heat, they start to fry—
Their flavor gets sour and dry.
He hopes for rain and sun in balance
Until autumn makes its cool entrance.

Early fall is far the best
For the annual grape harvest.
Amos calls his pals from the herd
To help him in the vineyard.
They all pitch in with the labor,
Knowing that their neighbor—
The prime wine-maker in the county—
Will share his fine bounty.

What a sight and sound
As the rhinos make each round,
Bringing grapes to the vat
Big bunches—juicy and fat.
When the picking is all done,
The wine-making gets fun!

Who is better suited, I ask,
For the next strenuous task
Of squeezing the thick juice,
Setting its goodness loose—
So drinkers can put it to use?

Who will not just lightly tromp
The mush, but thoroughly stomp
And press it in a frenzied romp?
Who better than a herd of rhinoceros,
Wild, singing, and boisterous,
Squashing and squishing while turning dark red
And a little dizzy in the head?

And now, out of the vats, everyone!
The harvest dinner has begun!
Amos brings out last year's wine
(The gang agrees it's divine.)
Next day, the vats are drained,
The juices get thoroughly strained,
Into oak barrels to age—
The tricky but crucial stage.

By spring, the vintage is ready to bottle.
Production goes into full throttle.
The rackety clackety bottling machine
Keeps the process surgically clean,
Adding a cork, then a label
So when you pour it at your table
You'll know this wine is *ordinaire*—
Which means it's good but not rare.

For me and the common herd
The wine of Amos is the last word:
Magnifique in its ferocity:
The essence of rhinocerocity.

BIGGIE DOG AND LITTLE PUP

"My time, your dime—what's up, Little Pup?"
Biggie Dog said on the phone.
"Some slime did a crime, beat me up,"
Said Little Pup, "and stole my bone."
"Did you snarl and growl, Little Pup,
Or cringe and howl?
Did you roll and groan, or hold your own?
Saying no to a bully—trouncing him fully—
Is a skill to hone.

I'll bring home your bone now,
He'll leave you alone now,
But we all have to do it—
Learn to get through it—
To live a dog's life full-blown.
That's my advice, Pup, you set the tone,
You can do it on your own!

THE HOUSEGUEST

Down at our house in the ocean
My old friend caused a commotion.
Fred might have helped with the chores,
But he proved to be one of those bores
Known as the houseguest
And he chose just to rest.

With eight arms, one might think
Fred could have wiped the sink
He might have strove
To clean the stove
Or swept a floor—plus five things more.

"Fred is here for a week's visit,
I'd told my wife—that's not too long, now is it?"
But she soon got fed up
And was ready to send Fred back up.
"The old blob needs a job"
She said. "He even annoys
The kids—he juggles their toys!"

But mostly Fred stayed in his room
Lolling in the silty gloom
With hours and hours of TV
On channels that weren't free,
A steady stream of briny soaps
(Which are only for dopes.)

So I finally said, "Old buddy, Fred,
Show me that you're well-bred.
It's time to get out of bed.
Enough AquaCable—
I know you're able.

Poor Fred, glassy-eyed
Meekly replied
"You've put up with this old Wuss
Of an Octopus.
I just needed a pause
From wrestling with fins and claws,
My daily grind.
You've been so kind—
You're a grand family
You've treated me dandily."

So he bought a new toy for each kid
And my wife got a smoked squid.
But his housegift to me
Was a toxic waste:
He left me his mindless taste
For the soaps on TV!

BAD ANDY BEAR

The bears all say
"There, you see,
Plain as day,
It's Bad Andy."

Always in trouble,
Messy, clumsy
Punishment double,
Bad Andy.

"She's oafish and lazy,"
The bears say,
"Plain brain-hazy,
That bad Andy.

"She knocks hives over,
Spills honey,
Crushes clover,
Naughty Andy"

"No, no,"
Say her mom and dad,
"She's not bad—
Just slow Andy.

She tries her best
Not always to be
An unbearable pest,
Our Andy."

But one day,
She ran away—
Misunderstood Andy.

Suddenly free,
Out on a spree,
She chased hikers
And mountain bikers—
Rambunctious Andy.

She growled, stumbled,
Scraped her knee,
Rolled and rumbled,
Runaway Andy.

She was full of sass
'Til it came to pass
As a camper fled,
Feeling sad, Andy said—
"Is this really, me—
Angry Andy?

"But wait! What shines?
What could this be?"
Look what she finds—
Put them on,
Curious Andy!

Holy molasses—
A pair of glasses!
And suddenly,
She could see—
Far-ly, near-ly, crystal clearly,
Sharp-eyed Andy!

She scooted home
Filled with glee
Proudly to shout
"Look at me!
New Andy!"

No more
Crushed clover
Spilled honey—
Clumsy days are over.
Happy Andy!

DOOZER OF THE DEEP

A man 'o war is also called a medusa—
Fine names though I choose a
Better way to describe what I'm seeing:
This soft-membraned, ethereal being,
My jellyfish friend Doozer.

He's a dangly, slow-motion cruiser,
An ocean parasol who likes to save
His strength by using the wave
Of his open-shut umbrella stroke,
Towing his tentacles—a graceful slowpoke,
A ballet dancer with the pace of a barge.

But beware his unseen electric charge,
A sudden ballistic, snap-zapping flash
That turns the careless into scaly hash—
Delicious, deep-fried, Doozered dishes.

So when you're swimming with the fishes,
Don't be a snoozer-
Watch out for Doozer,
He's a handsome bruiser.

BUG THUGS

Where backscratchers are souvenirs
They tend to come with sun that sears
Which often means a lot of bugs—
Keening, zizzing, biting thugs
Who always attack
Where you can't strike back.
So if you're itchy, never travel
To a place where on your arrival
You need a backscratcher for survival

MEAN CUISINE

Most he-goats are called Billy
But this one is not.
He answers to William
Which suits him a lot.

As a kid he was so hungry
He gave his mom a fright:
His kooky eating habits
Kept him up all night.

He'd throw odd foods together
To make a shepherd's pie:
Old shoes, and bones, and rubbish
Crusted with moldy rye.

William earned a chef's hat
But who could eat what he cooks?
He learned his art the odd way—
Digesting own cook books!

His daily barnyard special
Generates alarm:
A tin-can omelet of rotten eggs,
With spaghetti of sweater yarn.

It's health food, William argues
Yet none of his friends are listening,
His famous oven-cleaner flan
Still has their poor mouths blistering.

His weird fast-food concoctions
Make all the critters shudder,
Clock parts, fish eyes and nettles,
Stir-fried in rancid butter.

But William, a clever devil,
Always dines like a king—
When scaredy-goats don't dare to share,
He gets to eat everything!

IL GATTO

An Italian **cat** is *il gatto*
Their word for **big** is *grosso*
For **fat** they say *grasso*
And for **very**, *molto*.
When something is **bad**,
They shout, *Cattivo*!
And **is** is *è*
Now you can say
The Italiano way:
Il grosso gatto cattivo
È molto grasso—
The big, bad cat is very fat!

THE INCHWORM SPRINT

William, Ted and Thomas
Of the racing family Inch
Are off! Who'll win? Why, Thomas will,
That'll be a cinch!
He's big and strong, but look! He's down,
He buckled in a pinch!
Now William's leading—wait! He's gone?
He's breakfast for a finch!
So here comes Teddy, ready, steady—
The trophy will he clinch?
He's on the home stretch
Last, but first:
The winner: young Ted Inch!

THE TICKLING DINGO

I know a dingo named Dingle
Who loves to mix and mingle
With kids whose bare feet
He finds it a treat
To lick with a tickling tingle.

They twist with squirms and squiggles
As his nose on their toes he wiggles,
Then fall on the floor
Hooting for more,
Lost in an uproar of giggles.

FUNNY BUNNY

A rabbit I know named Sunny
Tells jokes that are screamingly funny,
And once you have seen
His standup routine,
You'll agree that he's one funny bunny.

78

He's a riot on rats and mice,
Toward cats he's especially not nice,
But everyone laughs
To see their own gaffs
Mocked slyly with humor and spice.

He loves a wicked lampoon
Of the noisily thieving raccoon
And then clowns around
To bring the house down
When he bays like a dog at the moon.

No one is safe from his wit
Save one, and she'd leave in a snit—
His wife, Mrs. Bunny
Who thinks it's unfunny
To hear herself teased in a skit.

Sunny helps everyone see
How silly we creatures can be.
So we laugh at each other
And hope there's another
Good joke about you
But not me.